I Am A
SIMPLE MAN
With A
SIMPLE FAITH
Who Added All the Junk?

I Am A
SIMPLE MAN
With A
SIMPLE FAITH

Who Added All the Junk?

JOHN H. DUMKE SR.

ARPress
ILLUMINATING IDEAS.
EMPOWERING VOICES.

ARPress
45 Dan Road Suite 5
Canton, MA 02021

Hotline: 1(888) 821-0229
Fax: 1(508) 545-7580

Ordering Information:
Quantity sales. Special discounts are available on quantity purchases by corporations,associations, and others. For details, contact the publisher at the address above.

Printed in the United States of America.

ISBN-13:   Softcover   979-8-89330-605-7
            eBook   979-8-89330-606-4

Library of Congress Control Number: 2024900572

TABLE OF CONTENTS

Luke 10:21 In that hour Jesus rejoiced in spirit, and said," I thank thee, O Father, Lord of heaven and earth, that thou hast hid these things from the wise and prudent, and revealed them unto babes: even so, Father; for it seemed good in your sight."

Matthew 15:3 But he answered and said unto them, "Why do ye also transgress the commandment of God by your tradition?"

Mark 7:7 "How be it in vain do they worship me, teaching for doctrines the commandments of men."

Mark 7:13 "Making the word of God of none effect through your tradition, which ye have delivered: and many such like things do ye."

Matthew 18:3 And said, "Verily I say unto you, except ye be converted, and become as little children, ye shall not enter into the kingdom of heaven."

INTRODUCTION

I am a simple man. I have no college degree, in fact until I was 54 years of age, I did not even have a GED. I left High School when I was 16, having just finished my sophomore year and struck out on my own, and boy did I strike out, time after time, after time. But I never gave up. You see, I had a secret. God had a job for me, a task I was to complete before I would be called home. And God was going to make sure I finished my course no matter what He had to do or allow to be done to me. God never fails. For most of my life I did not know I had this secret, but God knew. Then one day He revealed it to me, and finally my life made sense, and I rejoiced.

I am the son of a Pastor. I accepted Jesus into my heart at age 7, then at 18, I accepted Gods call on my life, but did not follow through. God remembers those moments of contrition and keeps moving us to the goal. Then at age 38, I truly turned my life over to the Lord. Immediately, everything turned for good and we lived happily ever after! No, it does not work that way. When you give your life over to the control of God, He begins a work of forming you into the image of His Son, Jesus. Sometimes it is not very pretty or comfortable, because he must chip all the lusts of the world and its systems off us before we can be the perfect Jesus look-alike, which will occur when we step into Heaven, Hallelujah! The transformation process takes time because we keep trying to hold onto all the rubbish of this world, and if He must allow us to go through some tough times to accomplish His goal, He will. If you are like I used to be, prideful, stubborn, with an "I can do it on my own!" attitude, it may take a lifetime for God to get through to you. But He is patient.

It is interesting that Adam and Eve were created by God the creator, (we know Him as Jesus), as God look-alikes in the Garden of Eden, Man made in God's image (Genesis 1; 27). He is now recreating us in His (Jesus) image. When people commune with us it should feel like they are communing with Him, Jesus.

One day when I was 55 years old, I had this terrible feeling that my life was not going to amount to anything, that my life was nearly over. I heard God say: "I can do more in your life in one year, than you can do on your own in a lifetime." I said, "I am ready, Lord, do your work on me!" The first thing He did was instructed me to do was write a book on marriage, and He even gave me the title. The Majesty, The Mystery, and the Mission of Marriage. It was published in 2020.

Year 2018 was my 40th anniversary of committing my life, spirit, soul, and body, to the service of the Lord. I call the last 40 years, my wilderness experience, and I can see the comparisons to the Israelites' wilderness experience. There are so many similarities. (I see a book there.)

They had some successes, so did I. They had some defeats, sadness, depression, times they wanted to give up, so did I. The beauty of it all is God is patient, He loves us and will take all the time necessary to bring us to the fullness of what He has prepared for our destiny. As it was for the Israelites, so it is for me now, the time has come to enter the Promised Land!

I have found that most instructional books are written to make the reader read to the end to learn the crux of the book and to receive the answers they were looking for. It is as if the authors want to build their story brick by brick, as if they were building a house, then when they install the roof, they tell you about the chest of gold sitting in the living room. We are going to reverse that order. First, I will show you the chest of gold, then build the house around it to prove its value. By the way, this is the formula Einstein used to validate his theory of E=m2.

OK, are you ready?

Here is the chest of gold!

John 3:16 For God so loved the world that he gave his only begotten Son, that whosoever believeth in him should not perish, but have everlasting life.

John 3:17 For God sent not his Son into the world to condemn the world; but that the world through him might be saved.

OK, that settles the issue of God's love toward us, doesn't it? Now what are we to do in order to receive His love?

Romans: 10:9 That if thou shalt confess with thy mouth the Lord Jesus, and shalt believe in thine heart that God hath raised him from the dead, thou shalt be saved.

Romans: 10:10 For with the heart man believeth unto righteousness; and with the mouth confession is made unto salvation.

Romans: 10:11 For the scripture saith, Whosoever believeth on him shall not be ashamed.

Romans: 10:12 For there is no difference between the Jew and the Greek: for the same Lord over all is rich unto all that call upon him.

Romans: 10:13 For whosoever shall call upon the name of the Lord shall be saved.

God so loved us that He gave us a gift that He alone could give. Through the death and resurrection of His Son, Jesus Christ, He paid the penalty of our sins, (death), then threw our sins into His sea of forgetfulness. He does not remember them anymore!

What must we do? Two things.

First and foremost, humble yourself before Him, confess you are a sinner, ask to be forgiven, and accept His free gift of salvation, and receive His righteousness.

Second, and equally important, confess with your mouth the fact that you are now a child of the most high God, and a Disciple of the Lord Jesus Christ. The reason confession is so important is that the words you speak have power. It was by words that God created our world and the entire universe. He gave us the power to create our world the same way. Be incredibly careful with what you say. You will eat your words, or the result of them. Awesome!

Please notice this is not something you say flippantly, like saying; "Isn't this a nice day?" No, it must come from the heart, as a commitment of belief. When I tell Nita Raye my wife, "I love you." It is a heartfelt statement. Every fiber of my being rejoices in my love for her! I confess and believe what I have said to be true. When I committed my life to God through the blood of Jesus, I was serious, and by faith, I joined the family of God and enjoy all the benefits of relationship as a son of Almighty God, and a Disciple of the Lord Jesus Christ.

Interestingly, this same fact or formula is stated in what I call a universal law established by God.

Genesis 11:6 And the LORD said, Behold, the people is one, and they have all one language; and this they begin to do: and now nothing will be restrained from them, which they have imagined to do.

And as a capstone, Jesus stated this in Matthew:

Matthew 21:21 Jesus answered and said unto them, Verily I say unto you, if ye have faith, and doubt not, ye shall not only do this which is done to the fig tree, but also if ye shall say unto this mountain, Be thou removed, and be thou cast into the sea; it shall be done.

Matthew 21:22 And all things, whatsoever ye shall ask in prayer, believing, ye shall receive.

So, what have we done? We have given the information of what you must do to be accepted into the Family of God, to have your sins forgiven, and to know assuredly, that when your time on earth is over, you will immediately be in the presence of your Father, Almighty God, and in the arms of your Savior, Jesus, the Christ of God, for all eternity. This is your chest of gold!

Here is a prayer you can use to give your life to God.

Lord Jesus, I confess I am a sinner, I ask you to forgive my sins, to cleanse me of all unrighteousness, and to receive me into your family, the family of God. I believe you paid the price for my sins by your death on the cross, and that our Father God raised you from the dead, to be our forever, Savior. Thank you, Lord Jesus, Amen.

Now get ready, we are about to build the house around your chest of gold, or in other words, you are about to receive the pattern and the proof of salvation, so you can lead others to Christ, and therefore, to safety from the judgement set to come on all the earth, and on all those who rebel against God.

CHAPTER ONE

MY FAMILY STORY

Not everybody was raised as I was, but here is my history. I was born on a farm outside of Sanborn Minnesota April 22, 1940. I was the third child. My brother Allen was the oldest, then came my sister, Darlene then me. It would be December 23, 1947, before our youngest sibling, David would come on board. Two of my mother's brothers were also farmers, living within a mile or so of us and each other. Dad farmed the ground, and mother had a coop full of laying hens, up to 1000, yes, that is not a misprint, 1000 or more. You could say they were doing well, were successful in their work. In fact, I found out later in life, through their hard work and diligence, they had paid off the note on the farm and now could live debt free! Then in the summer of 1943, as I recall my mother relating this, she and Dad were attending revival meetings in Germantown, at their Lutheran Church. After one of the meetings, Dad was quite moved by the Spirit of God, and throughout the next day all he could think about was what would he be willing to do for God's glory. Just the year before Mother's sister Loraine and husband Stanley, had felt called into the Lord's ministry, and that was on Dad's mind as he began milking his cows. Let me have my father tell the story in his own words.

"That evening as I sat down to milk the first cow, I looked up and saw a dove alit on the lower half of the barn door. A peace came

1

JOHN H. DUMKE SR.

over me and I smiled, enjoying the moment. Then I heard a question inside of me, like the Spirit of God testing me about my commitment to him. Yes, I had accepted Him as Lord, but now what?"

"What would you be willing to give up for me? Would you give me these cows if I asked you to?" I said, "Yes Lord." And the sweet peace increased over me.

"Allen, would you give me the flax field?" Now I was immensely proud of my fields of flax. There was a good profit in the crop, and everyone talked about how beautiful they were this year. This would be a particularly good year for the flax harvest.

I thought for a moment, then said: "Yes Lord, if you asked for it, I would give it." That sweet peace remained with me, I felt God's presence so strong.

"Allen, would you give me your Berkshire hogs?" I thought, oh boy that would be tough. My hogs are the envy of many of my neighbors. They are very profitable, and I have worked so long to build up my herd---but if God wants them.

"Yes lord, I'd give you, my hogs." The blessed peace was now a part of my being, then there was a long silence. I began wondering if I had really been having a conversation of commitment with the Lord, or if I was just imagining the whole thing. But the feeling of love and peace was like nothing I had ever felt before.

"Allen, would you be willing to give up the farm for me?"

What would I do? Where would we go? How would I support my family? "Oh no, Lord I cannot do that!!

At that moment, the dove on the barn door flew away. The peace and the love I had been enveloped in, disappeared, and I was devastated. I felt alone, abandoned, and afraid.

I finished the milking, took the milk to the separating hut, then went into the house and told Mae everything. We cried together, prayed together, then cleaned up and headed to the revival meeting at Church. I do not remember what was preached that night, I was anxiously waiting for the Altar call so I could go down there, get on my knees, give it all to God, everything, and get back under His peace and love. And that is what your mother and I did."

Mother told me this story many times. It became a part of our family lore or history. But think about it a minute. Dad asked some incredibly good questions. Yet God had all the answers, once the commitment had been made, they lived out their lives one day at a time.

I asked Dad one time when I was 16 years old if he ever regretted leaving the farm to go into the ministry. I was thinking about all my cousins, realizing that they all had a planned future because of the family farms, and I did not. He said: "I don't believe I could have lived with myself if I had not obeyed the call of God on my life."

<u>*A personal note on Dad and Mom's life changing decision,*</u>

Until I started writing this book, I never dwelt on the monumental decision Dad and Mom made at that time. They were going to "let it all go", everything they had worked so hard for, for so many years! And with nothing to lean on but the unction of the Holy Spirit, to follow a path they believed God had ordained for them? In the natural it was crazy! Dad was 34, Mom was 31, they had finally paid off the loan to purchase the farm, they had 3 children to care for, and now because of a "call" from God, they left everything behind and moved the St. Paul Minnesota to go to Bible School. Wow!

Life's decisions always look easier to do when they are contemplated before you must act, or after you have succeeded in the endeavor, then they are when you are in the middle of the rushing river of new and different events, swimming against the current to reach a far-off goal.

Think about it. One night you and your spouse are kneeling at the Altar, confessing your sins, believing God has forgiven you and accepting the call you feel so strongly, that you are willing to commit the rest of your life to the service of God in full time Christian ministry! You are willing to give up your life's goals and future, the plans you have worked so hard to accomplish, go to Bible school and become a minister of the Gospel? Wow, Oh the joy! The exuberance! You know it is all going to be good! Then you go home. The excitement becomes peaceful joy, and you sleep well, in the knowledge that you are in the middle of God's will for you.

Then the morning comes with all the chores, and work and the questions. How in the world are we going to do this? "I know we committed to you Lord, but now when we finally have the farming business going our way? Wow! This is tough! What do we do next?"

A thousand questions, no answers. Who can we talk to? Mom's sister Lorain, and husband Stanley are entering the ministry after Stanley had an encounter with the Spirit of God in a near accident. He was an over the road truck driver, and one day, driving in the mountains he entered a tunnel in good weather, but when he exited the road was covered in ice and his truck jackknifed and he knew his life was over. He cried out to God: "Save me Lord! I'll do what you want me to do." When he got home, safe and sound, he told Aunt Lorine what happened, and they got on their knees and committed *their lives to God's service. Mom said, "let's call them." They did and then they went to Mom's folks and told them. Grandma Schwanke said:" I hope you aren't doing this because of what Lorine and Stanley are doing." Mom said: "No mother we are doing it because we feel God's call on our lives like nothing we have ever felt before."*

What all they went through, the questions, the fears, the losses, the benefits, were all part of learning to trust God completely in all things.

In the fall of 1943, we moved to St. Paul Minnesota so Dad could attend St. Paul Bible Institute, Mom attended as well for a while. Both took jobs to pay the bills and believed God would provide for all their needs. Dad graduated in the spring of 1946 and was assigned to a Church outside of Hinton Iowa, on the condition that he would complete a 2-year standard college course at the college in Le Mars. Then he could be anointed as a "Reverend". Before he completed his 2-year course, one lady in the Church called him Reverend. He said: "Not yet, wait until the Evangelical United Brethren Conference makes it official." They did in 1948 after he completed his schooling and we were transferred to George, Iowa.

Each of us has a "God in my life story."

Again, here is mine.

1. Born 04/22/1940.
2. Born again in 1947 at age 7.
3. On my knees accepted my calling August 1958.
4. August 1978 committed my life to Christ.
5. August 2018 recommitted and entered my promised land for the rest of my life.

The rest of this book is my study guide through the scriptures and shows how that trip brought me from "saved" to total commitment.

As an historical textbook, we start with the birth of the Messiah, the savior of the world, who we know as Jesus, and carry it through becoming a child of the most high God. That means I laid my body on the altar of God and said: "Do with me as you wish. I will be obedient to your call and will live out my life humbly before you, standing on your promises, resisting the Devil, looking forward to the joy of being with you for all eternity!" Was this trek an even upward climb? No way! I had up times and down times, and my questioning times, but God is patiently moving us to a point of looking just like His Son, Jesus.

May I suggest you read this as a textbook, realizing that all Jesus did, was prophesied centuries before He did the actual deeds, and can be taken as fact.

But first a note about my friend David, and maybe you as well.

CHAPTER TWO

THE "ME AS MY GOD" PROBLEM
This is written for you and my friend David.

I have a friend who has heard and been exposed to the Gospel message for over 40 years, yet his intellect keeps getting in the way of the necessity of submission to Christ to receive the FREE gift of acceptance into God's family and His eternal Kingdom. My friend's acceptance of the concept in the Frank Sinatra song, "I Did it My Way" has become his hymn of belief and life. I want to spend eternity with him, and with his departed wife, in the light, life, and glory of God Almighty and our Savior, Jesus Christ, but I can't do it for him, I can only show the way.

He has seen Nita and I move from self-centeredness to submission and humility, from the god of self, to the one and only true God, and I know he sees the change, but his intellect keeps him from accepting Christ as the ruler of his life. Yet, I see a crack in the wall of denial, slowly but surely, I see him questioning his "Me first" beliefs and wondering if maybe John and Nita are right.

I cannot save him from himself, but God has chosen us to plant the seeds of right standing with God, so that before he leaves the land of the living, he will submit, commit and, as Paul the Apostle said: "Believe on the Lord Jesus Christ" as his one and only Savior.

I will continue to share the love of Christ with him, and continue to share the good news of redemption, and that Jesus is the one and only way of salvation. Believe and receive. Period!

There is no other way but to trust and obey.

CHAPTER THREE

The Emergence of the Anointed One

When you think about it, the story of what happened in the first century, AD, is amazing. The man who was Mary and Joseph's first born son named Joshua in Hebrew and Jesus in Greek, considered to be a bastard child, because his mother was pregnant before she and Joseph "came together," turned out to be the long-awaited Messiah, promised from the fall in the garden of Eden, and then all through the Hebrew Scriptures! All the elite men in Judaism had calculated the times and were looking for the anointed one. Yet, all the time He was right before their eyes, doing all the things the prophets had said He would do. They saw the miracles with their own eyes yet could not bring themselves to accept this man from Galilee to be the anointed one of God!

John: 7:41 Others said, this is the Christ. But some said, Shall Christ come out of Galilee?

John: 7:52 They answered and said unto him, Art thou also of Galilee? Search, and look: for out of Galilee ariseth no prophet.

It was this un-acceptance or unbelief that kept the people in Nazareth from experiencing the many miracles that other believing cities and towns did, from Jesus' ministry.

Matthew: 13:54 And when he was come into his own country, he taught them in their synagogue, insomuch that they were astonished, and said, Whence hath this man this wisdom, and these mighty works?

Matthew: 13:55 Is not this the carpenter's son? is not his mother called Mary? and his brethren, James, and Joses, and Simon, and Judas?

Matthew: 13:56 And his sisters, are they not all with us? Whence then hath this man all these things?

Matthew: 13:57 And they were offended in him. But Jesus said unto them, A prophet is not without honour, save in his own country, and in his own house.

Matthew: 13:58 And he did not many mighty works there because of their unbelief.

Here is what I see in this picture. God in His infinite mercy, grace, and wisdom maneuvered events to protect His Son from King Herod. We read that two years after Jesus was born, while they were still living in Bethlehem, (did Joseph keep his family there to avoid the gossip of the people in Nazareth?), the Kings of the East came to Jerusalem, to meet King Herod, to pay homage, and to enquire as to where the new King of the Jews was living. They told the King that they, the Wise Men, or Seer's, had seen the star in the east announcing the birth of the Messiah, the prophesied King of the Jews. What is hard for us to comprehend now 2000 plus years later, is that there was great expectancy and excitement in the land! It was the main topic of conversation with all the people, especially the priests and rulers. The long promised and prophesied Messiah, according to Scripture, was due to be born any time now. The time was fulfilled!

Where is He? And now outsiders had come to Jerusalem saying that they too had been notified of the birth!

They brought great gifts which Joseph and Mary used to supply their needs while they lived in Egypt, where the Angel of the Lord directed them to go, for King Herod, to protect his position as king, would send the soldiers to Bethlehem to kill all the male children of 2 years or less waiting for King Herod to die. Yet on their return, the angel of the lord denied their wish to go back to Bethlehem, and redirected them back to Nazareth, where Joseph knew the gossip would start up again. In retrospect, we see this plan as a great "cover" for Jesus. He was quite safe until his time to begin His ministry was to come into being.

God is so amazing! He has everything planned from the beginning of our lives to the end. He knows what the people of this fallen world are going to do before they do it, and He puts up barriers to stop them, then moves us so what was planned to harm us, actually protects and promotes us. When will we learn to just trust Him, instead of complaining? Rejoice always!

Another point of interest is that his friends, and even His siblings, could not, and did not believe Him to be the Messiah. Why? Because that would mean they were too dull of understanding to recognize Him earlier in their lives. I am sure you have seen the same thing happen to someone you knew, who one day after receiving Christ as Savior. and Lord of his or her life, did a 180 turn and became a new person, just like the Scripture said they would.

2 Corinthians: 5:17 Therefore if any man be in Christ, he is a new creature: old things are passed away; behold, all things are become new.

Pride is what kept them from humbling themselves and becoming like children so they could receive the good things God had stored up for them. Unfortunately, we make the same mistake sometimes! God forgive us!

Matthew 18:3 And said, Verily I say unto you, Except ye be converted, and become as little children, ye shall not enter into the kingdom of heaven.

Matthew 18:4 Whosoever therefore shall humble himself as this little child, the same is greatest in the kingdom of heaven.

Matthew 21:16 And said unto him, Hearest thou what these say? And Jesus saith unto them, Yea; have ye never read, Out of the mouth of babes and sucklings thou hast perfected praise?

Romans 10:8 But what saith it? The word is nigh thee, even in thy mouth, and in thy heart: that is, the word of faith, which we preach;

Romans 10:9 That if thou shalt confess with thy mouth the Lord Jesus, and shalt believe in thine heart that God hath raised him from the dead, thou shalt be saved.

Romans 10:10 For with the heart man believeth unto righteousness; and with the mouth confession is made unto salvation.

Romans 10:13 For whosoever shall call upon the name of the Lord shall be saved.

Here is the crux of the matter.

John 3:16 For God so loved the world that he gave his only begotten Son, that whosoever believeth in him should not perish, but have everlasting life.

John 3:17 For God sent not his Son into the world to condemn the world; but that the world through him might be saved.

God did the hard part, that which only He could do, then gave what He did, which was bringing mankind back into a personal relationship with Himself, to all mankind. What must you and I do? All we must do to receive this free gift is submit to His Lordship and accept Jesus Christ as our Lord and Savior. Period. Pretty simple, isn't it? Just don't add any junk!

CHAPTER FOUR

THE FIRST CENTURY A D

Another Perspective

The year was 3761 on the Hebrew calendar. There was nothing special going on, except in Bethlehem, where a group of Shepherds that spring had a heavenly encounter, or so they told everyone. They said a host of Angels told them that the Messiah had been born and they could see Him lying in a manger in Bethlehem! They left their sheep and ran into town and worshipped Him. They told their story to anyone who would listen, but after a while nobody paid much attention to them, that is until the year 3763 when a convoy of eastern Kings and Princes showed up in town to honor the new King of the Jews. A short time after they left, in the middle of the night, the boy and his parents, Joseph and Mary disappeared, just left without telling anyone. No one knew anything about their departure, until shortly after their disappearance King Herod's soldiers came into town and began killing all male children 2 years old and under.

Matthew 2:17 Then was fulfilled that which was spoken by Jeremy the prophet, saying,

Matthew 2:18 In Rama was there a voice heard, lamentation, and weeping, and great mourning, Rachel weeping for her children, and would not be comforted, because they are not.

Then there was the return to Nazareth, as directed by the Angel, which we discussed in Chapter two, followed by a period of silence until Jesus reached the age of 12, (year 3773) when under Jewish law He stopped attending the services at the Synagogue with His Mother, and began attending with His Father as an adult male.

Notice how Jesus followed all the laws and traditions as a good and Godly son, as proven by scripture.

Luke 2:40 And the child grew, and waxed strong in spirit, filled with wisdom: and the grace of God was upon him.

Luke 2:41 Now his parents went to Jerusalem every year at the feast of the passover.

Luke 2:42 And when he was twelve years old, they went up to Jerusalem after the custom of the feast.

Luke 2:43 And when they had fulfilled the days, as they returned, the child Jesus tarried behind in Jerusalem; and Joseph and his mother knew not of it.

It seems that Jesus stepped aside from His family to speak to the doctors of the law, or in other words He started His ministry by trying to get the leaders of Judaism to seek the truth concerning the Messiah. Then His parents found Him in the Temple:

Luke 2:49 And he said unto them, How is it that ye sought me? wist ye not that I must be about my Father's business?

Luke 2:50 And they understood not the saying which he spake unto them.

Luke 2:51 And he went down with them, and came to Nazareth, and was subject unto them: but his mother kept all these sayings in her heart.

Luke 2:52 And Jesus increased in wisdom and stature, and in favour with God and man.

I think it is noteworthy to see how Jesus, the second person in the Trinity, held His God-ness in abeyance while His human body took a normal time to mature, and to reach the 30th year of human life when according to Jewish custom, He was allowed to read Scripture and teach in the Synagogue. It was not that He did not have the knowledge to be able to teach, He already proved that He was capable to teach and to expound on the Scriptures when He was 12 years old. But rather, with the advancement of age, He would be accepted to a greater degree according to their custom.

If Jesus felt that was important in His ministry, perhaps we should do the same. Allow ourselves to wait for the appropriate time to expound on the word of God. Over the years I have seen too many well-meaning people enter the ministry before they were ready.

What did Jesus do during the first 30 years of His humanity? Well, we know both His earthly father and mother were aware of who He was, and teaching Him the Scriptures personally as well as in the synagogue school for Jewish boys was a given, and extraordinarily important as we can be sure the Holy Spirit of God hovered over the human Jesus from conception to crucifixion, just as He hovered over the earth in Genesis 1:2 and as He did over the throat of Hell, waiting for the three days and three nights to be completed while Jesus was in Hell paying for your sins and mine, and for every human from Adam to the last sinner at the end of the Millennium.

As a young Jewish boy, it was expected that he learns a trade, so no matter what may happen in the future, he would always be able to support his family. Since his earthly father was a carpenter, so would Jesus be. And as was noted above, He was subject unto them.

The years between the trip to Jerusalem at age 12, and the beginning of His ministry were filled with normal growing up activities. He had to take the position of the father of the family when his father died. His younger brothers and sisters were subject to Him as the leader of the family. He had to live with the never-ending stories of being a bastard child because his mother had become pregnant before she and Joseph had "come together" as husband and wife. Those kinds of things don't go away as you mature, they are attached to you like a leech. This is one of the reasons it was so hard for his friends and even his siblings to accept him as the Christ.

But before we get into the ministry of Jesus, let us look at the day it all started. The following is me taking literary license to see what happened:

CHAPTER FIVE

WHEN JESUS THE CARPENTER BECAME JESUS THE CHRIST

The Day Before

The widow brought a tray of cakes, some dates, and a pitcher of wine to her boys in their carpentry shop. She set it down and told them to take a break, rest and refresh themselves. The oldest son, Joshua, smiled and said, "Thank you mother." "Come on brothers, as father used to say, when mother brings a reason to rest, it must mean we need it."

The boys, men all, with the oldest just now 30 shook the wood chips and dust from their garments and sat down to eat. There was the normal shop talk of which jobs would be completed when, and what was coming up to be done, then almost as if a new train of thought were introduced, Joshua spoke to the next oldest, James.

"I will go to Gauis' place this afternoon to complete our agreement and to lay out the position of the barn he wants built. You need to start taking materials to him tomorrow. Our other work should be done before this Sabbath, so his can be started next week. Oh, and James, I have the books all brought up to date in father's desk. You'll know what to do to collect our pay at harvest time."

Joses said, "Joshua, you sound like you won't be here to help on the barn."

18

Joshua replied, "Well, if all other work is done by weeks end and if you two plus Simon and Jude will work together you can complete Gauis' barn on time without me." "And James just make sure mother receives my share of the profits, as well as her own."

With that, Joshua stood up, ending their rest and the conversation and went back to work on his project, which brought Simon to say, "He gets more like father every day. He won't answer our questions if he doesn't want to."

After the noon lunch Joshua left the shop and walked north out of town to Gauis' place. He always enjoyed these times of solitude. It gave him a chance to meditate on the word of God and to recite the Psalms. He also spent time in prayer, sort of walking and talking with God.

Gauis had been a good friend of their father and his son Lucius had been Joshua's friend for as long as he could remember. Although on this day Lucius was not home but on a trip for his father. Gauis said he expected him home on the morrow. Although they were Greek and their Hellenistic culture was evident in all they did and said, they nevertheless had accepted Jehovah as their God and were converts due to the life and witness of Joshua's father.

Gauis worked with Joshua to lay out the position of the barn and then they completed their arrangements. The barn would be paid for with grain at harvest time. This was the normal type of payment but that meant there were times Joshua and his brothers had to wait for payment due to poor crop yields or a prolonged rainy season. In fact, they had even had to help with more than one farmer's reaping just to make sure the grain made it into the barns before bad weather set in or they could not have been paid.

By the time Joshua got home the sun was setting, the shop was closed, his brothers were gone, and his mother had supper ready for him.

It seemed to him that she had prepared a special meal for this night, almost a feast. She waited until he was finished eating, then started a rather nostalgic conversation. It began with the often-related story of his birth; how incredibly special he was and the joy she had experienced being his mother all these years. There were pauses when each in their own way mused on the past. There was laughter at some of the silly things they had experienced and some of the joys. Joshua interjected his thoughts and perspectives in a way he could not remember doing before. His mother seemed to particularly enjoy his comments. She continued through each phase of her life recalling the trials and triumphs ending with the day she became a widow. She sighed then with a loneliness only known to those who have lost a loved one.

Joshua listened, letting the evening unfold. It seemed to him she needed to do this just now, and perhaps, just perhaps, he needed to as well.

Does she know? Does a mother know when her son is about to leave home?

At last Joshua arose and said, "Mother I need to walk awhile I feel a need to pray." he hugged his mother, wrapped his cloak about his shoulders and disappeared into the night.

Well after midnight, the front door creaked, and Joshua quietly slipped over to his sleeping place. As he spread out his mat a low moan escaped his lips and he groaned obedience, "Yes Father, I will. I know it's time."

His mother awoke with the door creak and then heard her son's prayer, spoken in pain. She quietly arose, opened a drawer, and removed a package. She laid it on top of the chest her husband had made so many years ago as a wedding present.

She lay back down to await the morning and her son's announcement. Then she whispered her prayer.

"Yes, Lord God, I know it's time. Thank you for lending him to me. I give him back to you now." It seemed as if a sword pierced through her own soul as she wiped the tears from her eyes.

Sleep did not come to either of them that night, only an occasional drifting in and out of a twilight rest until morning.

It was time.

CHAPTER SIX

THE MORNING THAT CHANGED THE WORLD

Joshua awoke from one of his twilight dozes but waited to open his eyes. It was that frozen moment in time just before the darkness of night was required to flee, chased by the rising sun. It was his favorite time. The rooster would crow the signal for all God's singers, the birds, to try to outdo each other singing praise to their creator. To open one's eyes now seemed to him to profane the moment. The other senses would be subdued if sight could reign. How could he smell the dawn if his eyes were open? It was as if God made special air, brand new air, for smelling at dawn. And the sounds of dawn! Of course, everyone heard the birds. The soft tweeting of a summer's afternoon that could lull a shepherd to sleep, came from the same throat as the screaming of dawn. They sounded like an orchestra tuning up before playing the concert of daytime melodies. The other sounds he listened for were the gifts of patience at dawn's first light, the insects' sounds, some nondescript, others musical. He listened for the cows asking to be milked, the she goats with the same request, the bleating of lambs wanting breakfast, the braying of a donkey and the distant cry of a hawk on the wind searching for food to feed its young. Each animal in turn announced its entrance into the world of awareness.

Then there were the mother sounds. He wondered if he had ever in his life awakened before her. In thirty years, he could not remember *even one time. He knew she had already started a fire, made the dough, and had the breakfast cakes in the oven, he could smell them. When he sat down everything would be ready as it always was.*

Wait, not yet. Take one last breath. Inhale deeply. Live for one more moment in the breathless, sightless wonder of the sounds of dawn. At last, he opened his eyes to this new day. He was blessed with a window that faced east just above where he slept and as he did every morning, he stood before it to enjoy the rising of the sun.

"Thank you, Father, for again allowing me the joy of your presence and the glory of your creation." he stood for a long time this morning, absorbing the beauty, and drinking the nectar of dawn.

At last, he rolled up his mat, stowed it away, and stepped outside. When he returned, he washed his face and hands and prepared to eat breakfast.

"Good morning mother." he gave her a hug and kissed her cheek. Although she had been a widow for some time now, was still young enough and very attractive, she was adamant about not remarrying. Her children had encouraged her to find someone to spend her later years with, but her response was always the same: "Who could ever replace your father!" Finally, the children gave up, honored her decision and no one mentioned it anymore.

Her daughters had all married and were busy starting their families as had her sons, all that is except Joshua. Now it was just mother and son, and they had drawn even closer to each other.

One element of their earlier family life continued. Their mother insisted on the "boys" having lunch with her each day since the carpentry shop was connected to her house and it was the family business. It made her feel like they still lived at home.

Now as Joshua sat to eat with his mother, they bowed their heads and Joshua prayed.

"Almighty God, Jehovah, who provides all things for life, we honor you, we give you glory. We pray for your will to be done in our lives and hearts even as you have purposed in heaven. Supply all we need for this day. Forgive us as we forgive others. Lead us in the paths of righteousness and deliver us from all evil. We give you all praise and honor for ever and ever, amen."

As Joshua began to eat, his mind recalled all the mornings of all the years they had eaten together as a complete family. Father, mother, and a house full of children. Where had all the years gone? When he was a child it seemed, he would never be a man. Now as a man, it seemed he had never been a child, that childhood had been a dream. Such is life bounded by time, he mused.

Recalling his childhood, he remembered traveling a great deal. He supposed, now that he was older, the trips had been much harder on his parents than they had been on him. But even now he found little pleasure in those memories. He enjoyed life much more after they settled in their village and the carpentry shop was opened. Some of his clearest early memories were of being in the shop with his father playing in the wood chips, and later learning the trade with his father's guidance. While they worked on the different projects the conversation was always directed to first include, and then be dominated by the scriptures. His father knew more scriptures and could recite more of them for his children's benefit than any man Joshua had ever known.

As was the custom, at the age of 8 he began his instruction at the Synagogue and had shown an extraordinary interest in the Torah. How he loved the stories of the history of his people, especially the settlement of the promised land. However, no matter how exciting those adventures were there was no question that the writings in the book of Psalms were his favorite. Over the years he had become a very learned expounder of the scriptures and was called upon many times to read in the synagogue. Now that he had reached the age of thirty, he would be asked to teach in the weekly assembly as well.

His mind seemed to be continuing the nostalgic travels of last evening only without the interplay of conversation with his mother.

He recalled his bar mitzvah, his first trip to the Temple in Jerusalem with his parents, his questions to the priests and each trip thereafter. He reviewed his life in a panorama of times and events not stopping until today.

His mother, noticing his silence spoke first.

"Son?"

"Yes mother."

"Is everything alright?"

"Yes mother. The business is going well. Jude and James will be here soon and will finish Eli's plow today. Samuel's yoke will be done tomorrow, and they will start on Gaius' barn next week with Simon and Joses. Joshua continued to give an inventory of the planned work of the business, not that she would be personally involved but rather to reassure her that her income from the business would be sufficient to meet her daily needs.

Again, there was a long silence.

Finally, after he was finished eating, he leaned back a bit and with the start of a frown on his brow he said, "Mother. Today I must be about---

Mary interrupted him with, "I know son. I have known for some time. I have been waiting for you to tell me. Wait here a moment for your mother's sake. I have something to give you before---" with that she left the room and went into her sleeping quarters and emerged with her package of love. In anticipation of this day, she had woven a one-piece cloak of white linen for her son. Oh, how long and tedious this labor of love had been, but worth it all now as she presented it to him, holding it out in front of her like an offering to God. He took it carefully unfolding it and letting her help him drape it over his shoulders.

"Son, you will need this against the cold of the night."

Joshua turned his back, so she could adjust the cloak and to hide the tears in his eyes. Had any mother ever loved a son as much as his loved him?

My mother. God's love was greater true, but when I look into her eyes, I see his love shining through.

"Mother, I don't know when---"

She interrupted again, "God knows. I'll be here when you want to see me. I've always known this day would come. I've never feared it, though it seems to me to have come too soon. I'll miss you very much, but I'll see you again. For now, I know you must do what Jehovah has called you to do."

Joshua put his arms around his mother, held her close for a few moments, and thought, "Why does this woman of strength seem so frail now?" then he turned and walked out the door. He did not look back. He walked through the town seeing things that had gone unnoticed on other days but now were things he wanted to remember. He drank in each scene and each memory, savoring it and saving it for future recall.

He climbed the hill out back of the village and as he had done so many times in the past he looked out over the pleasant land.

Joshua had become fluent in Hebrew, Aramaic and Greek due to the location of their village. Unique in time, their village stood at the crossroads of ancient trade routes from Tyre and Sidon on the west and old caravan roads from Damascus on the northeast. They were a halfway house between Damascus and Egypt, Antioch, and Jerusalem. Here competing cultures met, brought by traveling merchants with their goods, and travelers from Rome. Additionally, from the west came the caravans loaded with the cargo of the ships that unloaded at the seaport, Caesarea. King Herod the great had started building the city a half century ago and it took 12 years of intense labor to complete. He had spared no expense using the finest architects and engineers of his kingdom and meant for it to be a monument to Caesar. It had wide underground passageways for transporting carriages and pedestrians alike from the center of town to the magnificent beaches of the great sea. There were the theaters, the hippodrome and of course the marble temple Herod built to honor his god, Caesar.

From the north stretching down into Egypt, were the military roads bringing messengers with news from Rome. Sometimes they carried good news, sometimes bad but always with an effect on the people of the occupied lands of Rome's conquests.

Mount Carmel in the distance reflected the sun's rays and seemed to offer glory to God as a reminder of the day Elijah called down fire on the water-soaked offering and demanded of the apostate children of Israel, "If God be God, worship him!" From antiquity, the triumph of Elijah rang out as clear as the day the children shouted Jehovah's praises as they helped Elijah slay the 400 prophets of Baal. He looked to the north at Mt. Tabor and remembered the judge Deborah had sent Barak and 10,000 men against Sisera the captain of Jabin's army with his 900 chariots and a multitude of soldiers and God gave them a great victory. His heart felt the pain of loss as he recalled that King Saul and three sons died in battle against the Philistines on Mt. Gilboa to the south. His eyes continued further south to the area known as Samaria and wondered at the animosity between their two peoples. Samaritans, the descendants of the "mixed" multitude who came from Egypt with the Israelites, who walked with them for 40 years in the wilderness, were now shunned by them.

To the east was the sea of Galilee with its ring of hills appearing to protect it from the outside world. Herod Antipas, the procurator of Galilee, had built a palace for himself in the hills overlooking the western shore of the sea where the city of Tiberias was built as a tribute to the current ruler in Rome. Herod Antipas was the son of Herod the Great and half-brother of Philip the procurator of eastern Galilee and of Herod the Tetrarch of Judea.

It was about 28 years ago that their father had all male children 2 years old and under killed in and around Bethlehem to protect his kingdom from the possible birth of a new king of the Jews. Another great embarrassment to the Jews was that Herod and his son, the kings of the Jews were not even Jews, but Edomites, enemies of the Jews! A shudder shook his body as he thought on the cruelty of man to his fellow man.

Joshua turned his back on his country's past and started his descent eastward to the river Jordan. He was going to Bethabara on the other side of the Jordan, some 3-day's journey south not far from the city of God. He had received news from travelers out of Jerusalem of the prophet John, Jesus' kinsman, was proclaiming the coming of the "anointed one", the Messiah, and baptizing those who came to him repenting of their sins against God. His message was, "Repent for the Kingdom of Heaven is at hand!" When He heard of John's ministry, He knew His ministry was to begin.

He had planned to follow the river south staying away from crowds and off the main highway, the one Rome had built to connect Tiberias with Jericho, to have time alone with God, then to pass over to the east bank of the Jordan near Bethabara to find the prophet. However, as he approached the highway, he recognized his friend Lucius on the way home from the trip for his father. It would be an insult not to stop and greet him though he wanted to be on his way. The men greeted each other, Lucius always called Joshua by his Greek name, although no one else in town did. Joshua smiled at his friend's quirk. They visited about Lucius' just completed trip and Joshua's just begun one.

Then as the urgency was there to be on his way, Joshua ended their conversation with, "Lucius my friend, I must continue my journey, there is still a way to go before dark. I have an appointment with my kinsman John the day after tomorrow and must not tarry. Take care my friend until we meet again." he hugged his friend and turned to go. Lucius called after him, "Peace, and may our God prosper your way, my friend, Jesus!"

CHAPTER SEVEN

THE TRIP TO BETHABARA

Matthew 4: 13: *"Then Jesus came from Galilee to the Jordan to John, to be baptized by him."*

"Yes Father, I will do your will as a man, only as a man."

Jesus rose from his knees, stretched, and walked around for a while, not praying any longer yet in communion with His Father. Periodically the words, *"Yes Father"* would escape His lips punctuating the stillness of the night. Occasionally He would lift His eyes to stare fixedly at some distant point in the night sky which seemed to be visible to Him although there was nothing the naked eye could fasten on.

At last, He lay down and wrapped His cloak about Him for protection from the cool night air and thanked His mother aloud for her gift of love.

Sleep came for rest's sake, though He thought He would have preferred to continue His communion with His Father.

The first rustling of leaves moved by the per-dawn breeze which God sends to wake the warblers, His heralder's of day, woke Jesus to this day of destiny. As His eyes opened His heart and lips continued

His earlier communion with His Father. He had traveled about half the distance from Nazareth of Galilee to the place He would cross over the Jordan to where His kinsman, John was preaching and baptizing, a place near Bethabara. He had one cake left in His lunch pouch from home. After giving thanks He took a bite and searched for berries. Finding some, He picked a handful and enjoyed the blending of tastes. The sweetness took His mind back home and the memories of the preserves his mother would offer for breakfast. He thanked her aloud for the memories and love.

Jesus walked the last leg of his journey south to the road connecting Jericho on the west to the Jordan River and Bethabara on the East, with a determined step, a lively gate, and joined the crowd, unnoticed, coming to hear the prophet who many believed to be the Messiah. He listened to their conversations with interest. There were the ever-present Roman soldiers making sure no rebellion was afoot. And they all walked and talked together.

One traveler asked another; "Do you suppose this John is starting another revolt like the one started by that Judas of Galilee some years ago?"

Someone answered, "I don't think so. John talks of God and a Kingdom in Heaven and our coming Messiah, not rebellion against Rome."

One man asked no one in particular; "Is he the Messiah?" another answered, "He says no, but rather he is making the way straight announcing the Messiah's coming."

"Is He alive now? I mean the Messiah."

"Well John thinks so! He's looking for Him every day."

"What does the Prophet do? What does he say?"

"He preaches repentance toward God and doing good and not evil."

"Why is King Herod so angry with John?"

"Because John has criticized Herod for taking his brother Philip's wife Herodias, as his own and for not obeying the Laws of God."

"Doesn't John realize Herod could have him killed for what he has said?"

"I'm sure he does but that doesn't seem to affect him."

So, the conversation continued, one asking questions, others who had already heard John's message answering as they brought friends and family to hear what they had heard.

The air of excitement was thick with the expectation of the Messiah. No prophet had arisen for over 400 years in Israel. The devotees were hungry with a spiritual hunger that superseded even physical hunger, and it pleased Jesus.

The closer they drew to the prophet the greater were the number of the curious as well as the devoted. Today John was surrounded by his disciples, men who fancied themselves his protectors, men who had left their homes and livelihoods to hear his words and to be a part of the prophet's ministry, just as men have done for centuries when God raised up a prophet. The leaders of the Synagogue may hate them, even kill them, but they followed their prophets regardless the cost because they loved them, and it made them feel closer to God.

CHAPTER EIGHT

PREPARATION FOR MINISTRY

Jesus drew close to the river where John was baptizing and took His place in line with those who had been convicted in heart and desired to change their lives. He stood there waiting to be baptized. One after another John admonished then immersed the people in the river Jordan, then sent them on their way. He saw the tears of repentance, the joy of reconciliation and rejoiced in God his Savior.

Then Jesus stood in front of John. John knew who He was before He spoke. The Holy Spirit within him reacted just as He had at their first meeting while John was still in his mother's womb.

Luke 1:41 And it came to pass, that, when Elisabeth heard the salutation of Mary, the babe leaped in her womb; and Elisabeth was filled with the Holy Ghost:

John bowed before his Lord, held out his hand as if to prevent the baptism and said,

Matthew 3:14 "I need to be baptized of thee, and comest thou to me?"

He knew he had spoken the words, he had heard himself speak, but the whole scene was so surreal, unreal, here standing in front of him was the Son of God, his purpose for being, his purpose for life, for preaching; he for whom he had waited and hoped for was standing in front of him and wanted him, John, to baptize Him, God's Son in the muddy Jordan River like a common sinner! "No, it can't be so, Lord!"

Jesus smiling lifted John's head looked into his eyes and said:

Matthew 3:15 "Suffer it be so now; for thus it becometh us to fulfill all righteousness."

How could one deny a request from God's own Son?

"I baptize you in the name of the Lord God of Israel!"

As Jesus came up out of the water it seemed to John the world slowed down, and he saw each second of time elongated into minutes. Jesus rising, water falling, the sky opening, a dove landing on Jesus' shoulder, a voice sweet as honey yet thundering,

Matthew 3:17 "This is my beloved Son, in whom I am well pleased."

Then without a word, Jesus looked toward heaven, spoke words only He and God heard and walked away, never looking back, leaving John alone and longing to say or do something. For 6 long months he had been as one crying, nay, shouting in the wilderness of Judea, and in the wilderness of the hearts of God's apostate people, "Repent for the Kingdom of God is at hand!" And he believed it! Yet when Jesus the Christ arrived John was not prepared for His presence. Then Jesus was gone! John was left with an empty feeling and questions. Was he to continue preaching, to live out his assignment, his destiny? "Will He return to ask me to join His Kingdom administration? Surely the

King of Kings will want his prophet in His court. Oh, Holy Spirit, what do I do now?"

John 3:30 "Continue the preparation only now you must decrease, and He must increase."

Matthew 4:1,2 Then Jesus was led up by the Spirit into the wilderness to be tempted by the devil. And he fasted forty days and forty nights and afterwards he was hungry.

"Oh Father, I trust you. I care not for food for the body, my meat is to do your will and to finish the work you sent me to do. I will listen to your words, and speak them. I will watch what you do and do the same here. Your will be done in my life just as you purposed it in Heaven."

Jesus knew what would happen next. That old adversary the devil had waited until the body was its weakest and then he tempted God's Son with food, power, and earthly glory. When it was over, and Jesus victorious, God sent angels to minister to him and to refresh him.

"Thank you for coming."

"The Father sent us to strengthen you with bread from heaven and the water of life as we did for Elijah:

1 Kings 19:5 And as he lay and slept under a juniper tree, behold, then an angel touched him, and said unto him, Arise and eat.

1 Kings 19:6 And he looked, and, behold, there was a cake baked on the coals, and a cruse of water at his head. And he did eat and drink and laid him down again.

1 Kings 19:7 And the angel of the LORD came again the second time, and touched him, and said, Arise and eat; because the journey is too great for thee.

1 Kings 19:8 And he arose, and did eat and drink, and went in the strength of that meat forty days and forty nights unto Horeb the mount of God.

Jesus received this gift with thanksgiving and prayer.

"Thank you, Father. I commend to you my spirit to allow you to live through me, my soul and mind to think your thoughts and purpose to do your will. My body is yours to do with as it pleases you. When you desire, I will reject sleep and spend the night in communion with you, I only ask that you strengthen me to minister afterwards. When you show me what to do, I will do it trusting your power to perform each task. When you ask for my life, I will give it freely, willingly, and lovingly for love of our Man. Amen."

Three things encapsulate Jesus' message.

John 3:15 That whosoever believeth in him should not perish, but have eternal life.

John 3:16 For God so loved the world, that he gave his only begotten Son, that whosoever believeth in him should not perish, but have everlasting life.

John 3:17 For God sent not his Son into the world to condemn the world; but that the world through him might be saved.

John 3:18 He that believeth on him is not condemned: but he that believeth not is condemned already, because he hath not believed in the name of the only begotten Son of God.

Why did Jesus have to do everything exactly right. He gave us the answer. "Let it be so now; for thus it is fitting for us to fulfill all righteousness."

CHAPTER NINE

THE MINISTRY OF JESUS

And Jesus returned in the power of the Spirit into Galilee
(Luke 4:14)

J esus's ministry was to complete the plan of God, which was established from the foundation of the world, and along the way to do and say what the Father did and said, or in other words, when He heard God say something, He, Jesus was to say it. When He saw God do something, He was to do it precisely as He saw it done. This is what caused Jesus to spend a great amount of time alone and in prayer with the Father. This is a great lesson for us. We are to spend a great amount of time alone with God in prayer, for us to do and say what Jesus did and spoke. Amen! Let's break down what Jesus's mission was.

(1) He was to select, then call 12 men to be His disciples, to carry on the work of spreading the Gospel to the known world, after He returned to Heaven. He knew in advance that one of them would betray Him to fulfil Scripture and had already chosen his replacement. Think about this for a minute. Why would Jesus pick Judas if He knew he would betray Him? Was Jesus condemning Judas in advance? I believe the answer lies in the fact that God knows our hearts and He allows, does not cause, but allows a non-repentant person to live out

their destiny and uses that person to fulfil what God wants accomplished. God is always looking at the end "game".

(2) He, Jesus, was to minister to the people, train His disciples, He was to fulfil every prophecy concerning the Messiah's first coming, and, if you will, to prove without a shadow of a doubt to the religious elite, the doctors of the law, that He, Jesus the Nazarene, was indeed the promised Messiah, God's own Son come in human flesh to redeem the world. He was aware that the religious leaders would not accept Him. but He followed the plan He and the Father had laid out to the "dotting of every "I", and the crossing of every "T".

Matthew 5:18 For verily I say unto you, Till heaven and earth pass, one jot or one tittle shall in no wise pass from the law, till all be fulfilled.

(3) Jesus was to explain in detail the seriousness of sin, the necessity of redemption, and the glory of obedience to God, plus the rejection of all the added rules that were put in place to control the people, rules the elite seldom obeyed, called the Talmud. He demonstrated the Father's will by following the teachings in the Holy book, the Torah, the true instructions of God given through Moses.

Most importantly, He was instructed to fulfill the law, thereby bring to conclusion the dispensation of the law and to introduce the dispensation of Grace, which only He could bring in by His own death, (the price had to be paid by a perfect and spotless lamb, this final time, a perfect and spotless human being), then Christ Jesus was to rise again to introduce the new creation, born of a women, yes, but born again by the shed blood of Christ our God and Savior.

The idea of this new dispensation was abhorred by the hierarchy of the religious rulers because it took away their control of the people, their power and privilege.

Matthew 15:9 But in vain they do worship me, teaching for doctrines the commandments of men.

They lied to the Roman rulers and the general public concerning Jesus, even while some of their ruling members had accepted Jesus as the Messiah. Matthew 27:57. However God is the ultimate ruler, and He used their actions to catapult the truth of His words, spoken by Jesus and thereafter by His disciples to the whole world. Matthew 28:19. Without the advantages of radio, television, telephones, cell phones and social media, the 1st century experienced the greatest revival of all times and will stay in first place until Jesus' returns.

No reasonable person can deny that Jesus was, is now, and always will be the one and only Savior of the world, period! When you compare Him and His life to prophecy, you will find He fulfilled every prophecy spoken of the Messiah from the Garden of Eden.

Genesis 3:15 And I will put enmity between thee and the woman, and between thy seed and her seed; it shall bruise thy head, and thou shalt bruise his heel. to the last prophet in the last book of the Old Testament.

Malachi 4:2 But unto you that fear my name shall the Sun of righteousness arise with healing in his wings; and ye shall go forth, and grow up as calves of the stall.

Malachi 4:3 And ye shall tread down the wicked; for they shall be ashes under the soles of your feet in the day that I shall do this, saith the LORD of hosts.

Thus, we are assured that He will fulfill every prophecy concerning His 2nd coming. A child will believe when taught the truth, saith the scripture, and so should we.

To accept what has been taught so far, read your Bible. I suggest you start with the Gospel of John, the 4th book of the New Testament. It is generally accepted that the Apostle John wrote this Gospel, plus first, second, and third John as well as the book of the Revelation of Jesus Christ at the age of 80+ and approximately in the year of 95 AD. He had the advantage of growing up in a time when the Jewish nation was expecting the arrival of the true Messiah. Then he met Him and accepted Jesus as the Messiah and spent the rest of his life proclaiming the Gospel, the good news that God loves us, and Jesus died for us so that we, that is you and I, can come to Him in repentance and humility, accept and confess him as Lord and become a child of the living God. Hallelujah!

I also suggest you read the Book of Luke. Dr. Luke was a physician, a well-educated man who had accepted Christ, then in answer to an inquiry from a friend of His, a ruler by the name of Theophilus, he wrote an explanation of everything he had seen and heard concerning Jesus of Nazareth.

Theophilus expected his friend Luke to tell the truth, and that is why we find his gospel so detailed, almost like an attorney defending his conclusions. Perfect!

Most of the rest of the New Testament, except for those books that bear the name of their authors, were written by Saul of Tarsus, renamed Paul by our Lord. He was an enemy of the followers of "The Way", which would be renamed Christianity at Antioch, until he met Jesus on the road to Damascus. You have heard the story I am sure, but that encounter changed Saul to Paul, and from being an enemy of Christ to His greatest evangelist. Perhaps that is what is supposed to happen to each of us?? An interesting note about Paul is that virtually all his letters, now books of the Bible were written while he was in prison or under house arrest.

Question. If he had not been detained from his travels, would he have written any of these books? Would Paul have thought that just speaking in sermons was good enough? Sometimes God will place us in situations that cause us to accomplish His goal, that might not be very pleasant, but necessary. If Paul had not been in prison, would he have written all those letters of instruction we call scripture?

God has a plan to move each of us into our destiny. Sometimes the path is difficult and not to our liking, but if we will humble ourselves to His will, the result will be glorious! Thank you, Lord! The following is a word from the Lord when I was in great distress.

CHAPTER TEN

GLORIFY

I CHOSE TODAY TO GLORIFY YOU,
TO SING A SONG OF PRAISE.
TO SEEK YOUR PRESENCE AND YOUR LOVE,
MY HANDS, MY VOICE, TO HEAVEN RAISE.

IT MAKES NO DIFFERENCE WHERE I AM,
OR WHAT IS HAPPENING TO ME,
WHETHER GLADNESS OR SADNESS, PLEASURE OR PAIN,
IT'S IN YOUR WILL I SEEK TO BE.

I LOVE YOU LORD, I ALWAYS WILL,
I'LL FOLLOW WHERE`ER YOU GO.
AND IF MY ROAD IS STEEP AND HARD,
YOU'LL BE RIGHT THERE YOUR STRENGTH TO SHOW.

I AM SO BLESSED. I KNOW `TIS TRUE,
THAT NEITHER DROUGHT NOR FLOOD,
WILL STAY YOUR HAND OR BLESSINGS SURE,
FOR ALL WAS PAID BY CALVARY'S BLOOD.

AGAIN, I SAY, CHRIST
JESUS, MY SAVIOR AND MY LORD,
I CHOSE TODAY TO GLORIFY YOU,
GOD'S WORD, MY TWO-EDGED SWORD.

Copyright © 2017 John H Dumke

CHAPTER ELEVEN

The Gift of the Holy Spirit

I wrote with great intensity of the horror, the pain, and the terror of the experiences of Jesus from the Last Supper, through the Garden of Gethsemane, to the trial, sentencing and the crucifixion of Jesus. Followed by the glorious resurrection, in my book, "The Human Jesus in the Garden of Gethsemane", so I will not repeat it now. However, we want to look at what Jesus built and left for us to teach and maintain.

It is interesting to note that although the Disciples had spent the last three years with Jesus, had seen His miracles and in fact had performed miracles themselves through the power of Jesus' words as He instructed them, now that Jesus had died, been resurrected, showed Himself to them and had ascended into heaven while they watched Him leave, they were instructed by Jesus to return to Jerusalem and wait for the power of God to come upon them with the infilling of the Holy Spirit. Too many people not only now, but down through history have been teaching that the Baptism of the Holy Spirit with the speaking in an unknown tongue stopped with the death of the last of the 12 Disciples. We can consider that belief to be 3 things: unlearned babble, stupid, and of the Devil. Why would I be so unyielding in my opinion? Junk! Sometimes junk is the addition of beliefs, circumcision, the law. Sometimes it is the omission of the Baptism of the Holy Spirit and the gifts He brings.

Why would the giver of the indwelling of the Holy Spirit remove it after the first Disciples died? After all, Christ Jesus considered the empowerment of service to God and Him to be unattainable without the Holy Spirit indwelling the believer.

Luke 24:44 And he said unto them, These are the words which I spake unto you, while I was yet with you, that all things must be fulfilled, which were written in the law of Moses, and in the prophets, and in the psalms, concerning me.

Luke 24:45 Then opened he their understanding, that they might understand the scriptures,

Luke 24:46 And said unto them, Thus it is written, and thus it behoved Christ to suffer, and to rise from the dead the third day:

Luke 24:47 And that repentance and remission of sins should be preached in his name among all nations, beginning at Jerusalem.

Luke 24:48 And ye are witnesses of these things.

Luke 24:49 And, behold, I send the promise of my Father upon you: but tarry ye in the city of Jerusalem, until ye be endued with power from on high.

Acts 1:4 And, being assembled together with them, commanded them that they should not   depart from Jerusalem, but wait for the promise of the Father, which, saith he, ye have heard of me.

Acts 1:5 For John truly baptized with water; but ye shall be baptized with the Holy Ghost not many days hence.

Acts 1:6 When they therefore were come together, they asked of him, saying, Lord, wilt thou at this time restore again the kingdom to Israel?

Acts 1:7 And he said unto them, It is not for you to know the times or the seasons, which the Father hath put in his own power.

Acts 1:8 But ye shall receive power, after that the Holy Ghost is come upon you: and ye shall be witnesses unto me both in Jerusalem, and in all Judaea, and in Samaria, and unto the uttermost part of the earth.

We see in both the Gospel of Luke, the letter, he sent to Theophilus, a friend or acquaintance, that the Disciples who had spent the last 3 plus years deeply involved in Christ's ministry, were not to begin their ministry until they had received power to do the work, and that power would come from God through the Holy Spirit. While Jesus was with them, He, Jesus had the power of the Holy Spirit operating at 100% in Him and His ministry. He could, and did use the power, but also had the ability to transfer the power.

Luke 10:1 After these things the Lord appointed other seventy also, and sent them two and two before his face into every city and place, whither he himself would come.

Luke 10:2 Therefore said he unto them, The harvest truly is great, but the labourers are few: pray ye therefore the Lord of the harvest, that he would send forth labourers into his harvest.

Luke 10:3 Go your ways: behold, I send you forth as lambs among wolves.

Luke 10:4 Carry neither purse, nor scrip, nor shoes: and salute no man by the way. Luke 10:5 And into whatsoever house ye enter, first say, Peace be to this house.

Luke 10:6 And if the son of peace be there, your peace shall rest upon it: if not, it shall turn to you again.

Luke 10:7 And in the same house remain, eating and drinking such things as they give: for the labourer is worthy of his hire. Go not from house to house.

Luke 10:8 And into whatsoever city ye enter, and they receive you, eat such things as are set before you:

Luke 10:9 And heal the sick that are therein, and say unto them, The kingdom of God is come nigh unto you.

Luke 10:10 But into whatsoever city ye enter, and they receive you not, go your ways out into the streets of the same, and say,

Luke 10:11 Even the very dust of your city, which cleaveth on us, we do wipe off against you: notwithstanding be ye sure of this, that the kingdom of God is come nigh unto you.

Luke 10:12 But I say unto you, that it shall be more tolerable in that day for Sodom, than for that city.

Luke 10:13 Woe unto thee, Chorazin! woe unto thee, Bethsaida! for if the mighty works had been done in Tyre and Sidon, which have been done in you, they had a great while ago repented, sitting in sackcloth and ashes.

Luke 10:14 But it shall be more tolerable for Tyre and Sidon at the judgment, than for you. Luke 10:15 And thou, Capernaum, which art exalted to heaven, shalt be thrust down to hell.

Luke 10:16 He that heareth you heareth me; and he that despiseth you despiseth me; and he that despiseth me despiseth him that sent me.

Luke 10:17 And the seventy returned again with joy, saying, Lord, even the devils are subject unto us through thy name.

Those who say the power of the Holy Spirit was only for the anointed 12 Disciples perhaps didn't read this scripture. All who Jesus appointed and anointed received the power and did those supernatural things that Jesus did, through the infilling of the Holy Spirit!

"Well, what about after the death of the last Disciple?"

There have been down through the centuries and even today believers who are performing miracles in the name of Jesus, why?

Matthew 28:18 And Jesus came and spake unto them, saying, All power is given unto me in heaven and in earth.

Matthew 28:19 Go ye therefore, and teach all nations, baptizing them in the name of the Father, and of the Son, and of the Holy Ghost:

Matthew 28:20 Teaching them to observe all things whatsoever I have commanded you: and, lo, I am with you always, even unto the end of the world. Amen.

Jesus instructed all believers to be filled with the Holy Spirit, use His name, and do as He did.

The conclusion is, either Jesus lied, or we are to continue doing the works of God in the name of Jesus until He comes to take us home. Hallelujah!

CHAPTER TWELVE

S ome time ago I wrote an article when I heard of a denominational pastor was trying to start a new congregation here in southwest Omaha. I have reprinted it here.

Christianity isn't Kentucky Fried Chicken

Matthew 15:6-9

"So, for the sake of your tradition, you have made void the word of God. You hypocrites! Well did Isaiah prophesy of you, when he said: "This people honors me with their lips, but their heart is far from me; in vain do they worship me, teaching as doctrines the precepts of men.""

I read with interest the comments of a mainline denominational pastor the other day as he explained the marketing difficulties of starting and maintaining a church in today's American culture. We have so many diversions, so many activities that keep us from the eternal issues of life. He said the church must change in order to attract today's population. In a way he is right, the church must change. But his ideas lead people away from the truth, not toward it.

Christianity is not Kentucky Fried Chicken.

Christianity does not need a market study to determine its message. The "Church" with few exceptions has lost its way and its message. Jesus asked, "When I come again will I find faith?"

What is "its way?" What is the faith Jesus was talking about? These are not hard questions. The answers are in the Bible. We keep looking elsewhere because of rebellion and unbelief.

If the first century Christians could propagate the Gospel and change the world, there may be hope for us.

The Gospel or Good News is this:

Man could not reach God nor win His acceptance, so God did something about it.

John 3:16 "For God so loved the world that He gave His only begotten Son, that whosoever believed in Him should not perish but have everlasting life."

(2) Man has only two choices.

(A) Accept God's gift of salvation through Jesus the Anointed, (Christ).

(B) Reject God's gift.

Your decision will determine your relationship with God both in this life and for all eternity.

(1) You must accept Jesus Christ as savior and Lord on Grace alone. You must acknowledge that you can do nothing, and you have done nothing to merit your new relationship with God.

(2) You are now to allow the Spirit of God to live through you to love people into wanting to have what you have, peace, joy, and eternal security.

I read his comments with interest because if there ever was a time of other interests keeping people away from the Gospel it was in the first century with the pagan practices of competing religions which glorified and satisfied the flesh, the human senses. Yet during that time the mainly uneducated believers helped in turning the world upside down for God with the good news that Jesus was, is, and always will be Lord.

How did they do it? Look in the book of Acts.

If you want to build a church; heal the sick in the name of Jesus. Open blind eyes. Make the lame walk, and deaf ears hear, or in other words, preach the message of deliverance in the name of Jesus. You cannot build a building large enough to hold the crowds of people eager to get answers to their problems. You will not have a problem of marketing or maintaining, only of finding room to hold the crowds. Most churches today are little more than service organizations. They help people with the philosophy of man's wisdom instead of the power of God.

If you want to build a church, be a deliverer not an entertainment director on a cruise ship or in this case building.

Aren't all religions the same?

Won't we all spend eternity with our God? YES, AND YES!

EXPLANATION:

Religion is man's attempt to reach God. Therefore, by definition all religions are the same in that all are trying to <u>DO</u> something to be accepted by their god.

And yes, you will spend eternity with <u>YOUR</u> god, the god of your choice and your making.

Both of these questions can be explained with a common thread of thought and evidence.

The reason so many people believe all roads lead to God and heaven, is because all religious thought has a common beginning. That proves the obvious; "In the beginning God---" Not monkeys, not slime, but God.

Regardless of how many religions there are, or how many denominations, (see my definition of denominations on our website at www.rejoicetoday.com), there is the common beginning of God creating man in His image and likeness and giving him dominion over all of creation.

God set the rules for communion with Him. The creator directing the activities of the created. Man in turn, starting with Adam and Eve and continuing with Cain, Nimrod, and the infamous Tower of Babel, as well as countless others down through the centuries have attempted to circumvent God's commandments with their own interpretations of the rules.

In fact, what man has done in each religion and denomination is "created their god in their image and likeness." Man was created to be an under god, under only Almighty God and man has never forgotten his intended role, that of being a god. He wants to be god of himself and all he sees but God our Father will not allow it under this present curse. Man's answer to non-submission is to change gods. He simply designs a god to fit his beliefs and bows down to him. Then if in the course of time man changes his mind on what a proper god would ask of him, he changes again until he finds the god that best fits his lifestyle. Isn't that what denominations are doing when they try to fit the message to the current culture?

"So, for the sake of your tradition, you have made void the word of God. You hypocrites!"

And it is true you will spend eternity with YOUR god. There is only one true God. If your god isn't Him, then your eternity will not be spent with him. What is your definition of Hell? Mine is simply not being with Almighty God, His Son Jesus the Christ, and the Holy Spirit. Just knowing that you could have spent eternity in Heaven will cause the gnashing of teeth and uncontrollable pain and regret.

Knowing that there is but one God who loves you so much He sent His only Son to show you the way to His glory, doesn't it make sense to accept Him as your God?

Another especially important fact:

Almighty God never started a religion. He did not start what the Bible calls the Jew's religion. He is not the originator of the Roman Catholic religion nor the Lutheran, Baptist, Presbyterian, Assembly of God, Church of God, or any other denomination. Nor is He the originator of Islam, Hinduism, Buddhism or any other of the religions of the world. God is not religious! Man, in pretended piety, acts deeply religious, but not God.

God reached down to man and accomplished what man, through religion tries to do, but never can. God, seeing the futility of man's efforts to reach Him, sent His Son to touch man with His love and to put man back into a vital, vibrant, personal, intimate, relationship, like but better than the original relationship He established with Adam and Eve. We have a better covenant than the Israelites, so the Scriptures tell us, and better than the one with Adam, because we serve Jesus the second Adam with all His power and authority given to us to use here and now for the Glory of God!!! If you are steeped in a religion or denomination or doctrine, where you are trying to follow their rules to be accepted by God, you have missed God. Step aside, be Man, and let God be your God. He will draw you to himself and cause you to worship Him.

God created man to have an equal with whom He could have communion. I know that comment has a few people gritting their teeth. But look at the Scriptures.

Genesis 3:8 "And they heard the voice of the Lord God walking in the garden in the cool of the day:"

Almighty God calls Himself our Father. What father does not want a personal relationship with his child? Father God treats us according to our spiritual age. I treat our children, now all grown, differently than when they were small and inexperienced. Our Father does the same for us. But whether we are new babes in Christ or full grown He wants to talk to us and walk with us in an equal being relationship, not as a master to his dog. We need to accept who we are and what we are in the Father's eyes and start acting like children of the King!

If what I have just said is true, then how and why do false religions and various denominations grow? because each religion or doctrine feeds off the desires to be accepted by God and the fear of not being accepted by Him. How? If I can convince you that I know the way of salvation and others have missed it, I have my first convert to the First Church of What John Believes. I now have power over you and together we will work to find others who have lost their way and need someone to lead them.

Let us look at just a few examples.

The first break in the oneness of the early followers of The Way, comes in the glorious celebration after The Day of Pentecost, when every believer joined in food and fellowship with each other.

Act 6:1 And in those days, when the number of the disciples was multiplied, there arose a murmuring of the Grecians against the Hebrews, because their widows were neglected in the daily ministration.

The 12 Disciples stepped in and corrected an error, because they understood the importance of Oneness, as Christ had prayed to the Father for, and instructed them to be.

Acts 6:2 Then the twelve called the multitude of the disciples unto them, and said, It is not reason that we should leave the word of God, and serve tables.

The second attempt to create confusion we find in:

Acts 15:1 And certain men which came down from Judaea taught the brethren, and said, Except ye be circumcised after the manner of Moses, ye cannot be saved.

Acts 15:2 When therefore Paul and Barnabas had no small dissension and disputation with them, they determined that Paul and Barnabas, and certain other of them, should go up to Jerusalem unto the apostles and elders about this question.

When they arrived in Jerusalem to clarify the teachings, they were met by another group who had departed from the simple truth.

Acts 15:5 But there rose up certain of the sect of the Pharisees which believed, saying, That it was needful to circumcise them, and to command them to keep the law of Moses.

Acts 15:6 And the apostles and elders came together for to consider of this matter.

These are just the beginning of groups who wanted to add something to the simplicity of The Way, or Christianity.

All of us were brought up in some belief system, or denomination, and accepted what we were taught as children, then young adults. But have you ever asked the question: "why are there different churches when Jesus taught us to be ONE? Here is my answer.

Christianity means Christ Like.

First let us state the truth. God is able to find those whose hearts are pure, who love Him and who have accepted Jesus Christ as their savior.

It makes no difference what Church they belong to, or attend, as long as they have and continue to follow this admonition:

Romans 10:8 But what saith it? The word is nigh thee, even in thy mouth, and in thy heart: that is, the word of faith, which we preach;

Romans 10:9 That if thou shalt confess with thy mouth the Lord Jesus, and shalt believe in thine heart that God hath raised him from the dead, thou shalt be saved.

Romans 10:10 For with the heart man believeth unto righteousness; and with the mouth confession is made unto salvation.

Rom 10:11 For the scripture saith, Whosoever believeth on him shall not be ashamed.

I realize there are good people in all denominations who may disagree with this, because of teaching they have had from their youth, but it must be said. Christianity is not a religion! Neither God nor Jesus Christ ever set up a Religion or Denomination, From the earliest writings of Genesis on, this has always been about a Relationship each person needs to have with God the Father, God the Son, and God the Holy Spirit, period.

Whether you are a Catholic, or Protestant, or a member of a fringe group who tries to follow Christ, you are still required to establish this personal relationship with God through Jesus Christ.

Amazingly God sifts through all the foolishness of man's creations, finds the good and continues toward the end He alone sees and proclaims.

When my Father was the Pastor of the Evangelical United Brethren Church in George Iowa in the late 1940's, I had a friend Greg Winkle, who belonged to a different church. One year he attended our Vacation Bible School, and I attended his. On the graduation Sunday for our Church, Greg was treated just like the rest of us. However, when I attended the graduation service at his Church, I was not allowed to take communion, because I wasn't a member of that denomination.

58

Every denomination has their own set of dos and don'ts. I am reminded of what Jesus accused the religious leaders of His day of doing. I see our church leaders doing the same today.

Matthew 11:16 But whereunto shall I liken this generation? It is like unto children sitting in the markets, and calling unto their fellows,

Matthew 11:17 And saying, We have piped unto you, and ye have not danced; we have mourned unto you, and ye have not lamented.

It is interesting that Jesus called their kind of worship, "the Jew's religion," not their relationship with God the Father.

We must start each day with a prayer of thanksgiving for the immeasurable grace of God to look past our child-like foolishness of religious trappings and see our hearts, which for the true believer are focused on Him and Jesus our Savior.

ISLAM

This is a perversion of Christianity spawned by the abhorrence of the atrocities of some so-called Christians. They acknowledge Jesus as a great teacher but not as the Son of God. They accept Him but without power. They set up their founder as greater than Jesus. Muhammad was a terrorist who with his band of followers killed anyone who refused to believe as he did. He had nine wives the last one was just nine years old when he took her. Today we would call him a pedophile.

Why does this sick religion grow? Because many of the same tactics used at the outset are used today. Look at other parts of the world where Islam is forced upon people. The Muslims want us to believe the terrorists are radical Muslims and the true Muslims are peace loving people. This is a lie. True Islam teaching follows its founder, and it is violent and hateful. Think about this a minute. If the one true God is love and His Son came in peace to show the reality of what and who God is, then one who comes in violence and hatred is by definition His enemy or of the devil.

The kinder Islam we see today is simply a lie used to draw people into itself and away from the truth.

Some will say Christianity has a cruel history. Not true. Our founder never hurt anyone, never forced anyone to accept Him or the one true and living God, but rather through love, kindness and compassion demonstrated God's love to all mankind. Those acts of cruelty committed by religious people who called Christianity their religion were acting out of dogmatic zeal, not Christian love.

I heard John Osteen, an evangelist, say one day that a lot of uppity Christians were going to be very surprised by some of heaven's inhabitants. God is not bound by denominations or religions. There will be people in heaven that God judged by what was in their hearts not having had the privilege of hearing the Gospel.

There are Baptists and Presbyterians, Methodists and Catholics, people from every denomination who have been baptized, have taken communion, attended church all their lives but who will not be in heaven because they rejected God's gift, they followed their own self-made god. Remember we will spend eternity with the god we choose to worship.

Listen to the words of the hate mongers and you can tell what spirit moves them, a spirit of demonic dimension, or the Spirit of Love. There are those who call evil, good, and good, evil and there are those who will call me a hate monger for not accepting other points of view. However, telling the truth is not hate mongering and telling lies is not acting in love.

Jesus used the most scathing words when chastising the religious leaders, the clergy of his day, trying to shock the truth into them. That was the most loving thing He could do because they were on the road to perdition and were taking the multitudes with them.

Matthew 15:7 Ye hypocrites, well did Esaias prophesy of you, saying,

Matthew 15:8 This people draweth nigh unto me with their mouth, and honoureth me with their lips; but their heart is far from me.

Matthew 15:9 But in vain they do worship me, teaching for doctrines the commandments of men.

Jesus is called truth, light, and life. Therefore, those coming against Him either covertly or overtly are liars, darkness, and death.

Simple Christianity can best be defined as follows: Deliverance from the results of sin, (Hell), deliverance from continuous sin, (the sin nature), and deliverance from the effects of sin, (sickness, poverty, and premature death), and living now in the Kingdom of God at one with Jesus our Savior and our Father God.

True Christlikeness is God in human flesh demonstrating the love and deliverance of God to man again.

Let us review the truth.

John 3:16 For God so loved the world, that he gave his only begotten Son, that whosoever believeth in him should not perish, but have everlasting life.

John 3:17 For God sent not his Son into the world to condemn the world; but that the world through him might be saved.

OK, that settles the issue of God's love toward us, doesn't it? Now what are we to do in order to receive His love?

Romans: 10:9 That if thou shalt confess with thy mouth the Lord Jesus, and shalt believe in thine heart that God hath raised him from the dead, thou shalt be saved.

Romans: 10:10 For with the heart man believeth unto righteousness; and with the mouth confession is made unto salvation.

Romans: 10:11 For the scripture saith, Whosoever believeth on him shall not be ashamed.

Romans: 10:12 For there is no difference between the Jew and the Greek: for the same Lord over all is rich unto all that call upon him.

Romans: 10:13 For whosoever shall call upon the name of the Lord shall be saved.

Again, here is a prayer you can use to give your life to God.

Lord Jesus, I confess I am a sinner, I ask you to forgive my sins, to cleanse me of all unrighteousness, and to receive me into your family, the family of God. I believe you paid the price for my sins by your death on the cross, and that our Father God raised you from the dead, to be our forever Savior. Thank you, Lord Jesus, Amen.

Ok. You now have all the proof and the tools to be an ambassador of Christ, a proclaimer of the Gospel. Go do it!

Wait, one more thing! Aren't we to be ONE as God and Jesus are ONE?

John 17:20 Neither pray I for these alone, but for them also which shall believe on me through their word;

John 17:21 That they all may be one; as thou, Father, art in me, and I in thee, that they also may be one in us: that the world may believe that thou hast sent me.

John 17:22 And the glory which thou gavest me I have given them; that they may be one, even as we are one:

John 17:23 I in them, and thou in me, that they may be made perfect in one; and that the world may know that thou hast sent me, and hast loved them, as thou hast loved me.

If what Jesus prayed is true, and what His and the Fathers desire is, why are there so many divisions?

The following is how I see the development of denominations.

CHAPTER THIRTEEN

THE START OF DENOMINATIONS

The scene: *Somewhere in the heavens, directly over Jerusalem.*

The time: *Shortly after the Day of Pentecost.*

The actors: *Satan and several of his cohorts. And Pride.*

What an unholy crew, Satan the ruler of the underworld and three of his demon helpers, Complainer, Hater, and Death.

What they were watching from their vantage point of spirit infested air, was the sharing of assets among new believers in Jesus in the afterglow of first His resurrection and more recently the power promised to new believers through the indwelling of the Holy Spirit.

Complainer speaks first.

"I thought you said we won when you got the people to kill Him. I thought you said we had Him forever in the bowels of Hell. I thought— "(Not one of the demons or Satan himself can ever bring themselves to speak His name for fear of the power in that name.)

"Oh, shut up!"

Satan was distraught. He thought he had his enemy in his power. Over and over in his mind the events of what had become known as "Day Four" ran like a motion picture.

First the crucifixion, then leading the spirit of Jesus to Hell, locking Him up and watching Him suffer for three days and three nights. He and all Hell's inhabitants taunted Him endlessly for what He had done to hurt their purposes while He lived on earth. But then on "Day Four;" Even Satan had to admit it was quite spectacular.

In the midst of all the weeping and gnashing of teeth, Jesus sat quietly waiting for dawn. Suddenly a great, powerful, mighty rushing wind swept into Hell causing the very foundation to shudder! It went directly to the cell holding Jesus and entered Him! He who a moment before had sat so still stood up in the power of the Holy Spirit of God, having within Him all the power and authority in Heaven and earth and over all creation! He tore the hinges off the door and stood in front of His adversary, Satan and whipped him, exposing him to all the inhabitants for the toothless phony he was. Then Jesus took the keys to death, hell, and the grave away from Satan.

"I lost my keys!" It was all Satan could think of or say.

Now all that was left for him to use to defeat Man was deception. No more power only lies.

Jesus preached the world's shortest sermon to the captives in Abraham's bosom, saying simply, "I AM!" Then He led them to heaven.

Yes, Satan thought it was impressive. But it only made him hate Him more.

Satan's thoughts were interrupted again by Complainer. "What are we going to do now, oh great master." Satan heard that remark

65

and the sneer. He hated them all. But that was the question, wasn't it? What was he going to do to destroy Man now that Jesus through the Spirit of God had returned their power to them? Oh, how he hated them! Mankind, God's great creation made to rule the earth and everything in it. His world! He, Satan, had the right to rule taken away because of his pride of his own beauty.

"What to do? What to do?"

In the distance, but closing fast, came a black chariot pulled by black angry steeds causing great commotion and cloud dust flying in all directions. They stopped right in front of the assembly. Two footmen quickly jumped down and with great fanfare one blew a horn while the other opened the door to allow PRIDE to appear.

Pride, the only spirit having the ability to hide himself within himself, (have you ever noticed that prideful people never recognize themselves as proud?) looked at the group with disdain.

"Now what's the matter?" he asked. Satan tried to ignore him. Pride had always felt he deserve more honor than Satan, it was after all, he, Pride, who had caused the rebellion in heaven he had simply used Lucifer to accomplish his end, or so the hate filled argument went.

Complainer, Hater and Death all wanted to tell Pride what they thought about the new believers. "We are never going to get them now. They all love each other." Complainer said. Hater chimed in with "I hate them and their leader, but I don't know what to do!" Death asked, "How do we kill the God life?"

Pride sighed. "Has everyone forgotten what I have taught you over these long centuries? When you have no real power over Man you deceive them and cause them to destroy each other."

"And how do you propose we do that?" asked complainer.

"Watch me."

The group watched as Pride descended to the supper gathering of believers. They watched as he whispered in the ear of one of the women from Greece.

Acts 6:1 "there arose a murmuring of the Grecian's against the Hebrews because their widows were neglected in the daily ministration."

As Pride rejoined the others, he said rather smugly, "See how simple that was? Just suggest they do the opposite of what He told them to do. He said they should be one. We say divide them and we win. If we keep them fighting among themselves, they will be devoid of power and our influence will be greater than theirs."

"So how do we control them in all the different places they live?" Death asked.

"Use what is already in place. Each nation has a prince of demons in control of the area and can operate without interference as long as the people allow them to, and as long as the people don't claim the area in the name of Him."

"OK, OK, OK this will work. I can see it working!" Death was speaking again excited about the death of the new movement based on Him.

Hater had an idea. "We need to name the new divisions."

Satan warming now to the prospect of turning defeat into victory spoke. "Why not call them what we always have, Demon Nations?"

Complainer argued, "Nobody will follow a movement called Demon anything."

Pride sighed again and scolded; "Can't anyone think? Deception! Change a couple of letters and they wouldn't know the difference, but we will know they are singing our song. In fact, they will be calling for their own destruction and not even realize it.

Someone said, "Reverse the order of the N and M. They sort of look alike anyway. Call the divisions Denom nations."

Someone else mused, "There is something not right about that word. What is it?"

Pride said smiling, "The problem is I am not in the middle of the solution. If you put Pride in the middle of the word, it flows off the tongue like honey and I, Pride can hide in all their affairs. Denom I nation is just another word for division and when we separate them with divisions Complainer, Hater and Death can all work undetected, protected by me, Pride."

Fanciful story you say, but did it work?

The first denominations were called sects and yes it worked in the first century and it is working today.

"THE FIRST CHURCH OF THE CIRCUMCISION"

Acts 15:1 & 5

Vs: 1 And certain men which came down from Judea taught the brethren, and said, "Except ye be circumcised after the manner of Moses, ye cannot be saved."

"THE FIRST CHURCH OF THE CIRCUMCISION & THE LAW OF MOSES"

Vs: 5 But there rose up certain of the sect of the Pharisees which believed, saying, "That it was needful to circumcise them, and to command them to keep the Law of Moses."

Please notice the members of the sects were called believers. These were Christians who added their own rules or beliefs to the pure simple Gospel.

Acts 16:31 --- "Believe on the Lord Jesus Christ and thou shalt be saved and thy house."

If you are caught in the rules and doctrines of men, come out from among them, be freed by the Son of God, worship and seek Him and you will be found.

CHAPTER FOURTEEN

The following is part of a thought-provoking speech I will give on my Pod Cast or perhaps could give in your assembly.

<u>Why so many Denomination</u>

It is a privilege to speak to you today. My greatest joy is sharing what God is doing in the world with those of like mind and faith.

I have a question which each of us must answer and I present it to you for your consideration.

Why are you a Presbyterian? Or for that matter a Methodist, Catholic, Assembly of God or a member of any denomination?

Are you more comfortable here than at another church? Do you get along with these people more than some others you know?

I ask these questions because we have managed to create divisions where there was to be none. One people; a light unto the darkness of the world. Jesus prayed in the 17th chapter of John, "that they, (us), may be one as we are one." Certainly, this begs the question, why are we disobedient?

I believe the reason is that the enemy has taught us to be religious rather than relational.

Our relation to God began in the Garden of Eden and in reality, God has never changed His plan. Man denied the relationship through rebellion but God, the loving Father, keeps calling us back to Himself.

Let us look at the origin of religion. Let us see how the story line of religion has remained the same through thousands of years of history. It really would be humorous if it were not so sad to hear modern man proclaim the new thoughts and ideas of the "New Age" movement. There is nothing new about it except the current generation which adheres to its tenets.

The call of the serpent, God's enemy, remains ever the same, "Ye shall be as gods knowing good and evil." Adam and Eve were already gods or under rulers of all God created. What was enticing about this concept? The real desire was to replace God as their ruler, with themselves! How do we know that? Because that is exactly what Lucifer tried to do when he rebelled.

Isaiah 14:13 For thou hast said in thine heart, I will ascend into heaven, I will exalt my throne above the stars of God: I will sit also upon the mount of the congregation, in the sides of the north:

With Adam and Eve, he was trying to get God's greatest creation to follow in his footsteps. And he succeeded.

There is an old story about the leaders of three Baptist churches in a small town getting together for lunch one day. After they finished their discussion there were four Baptist churches in town.

Man does not want to be ruled. Jesus says, "submit." Man says, "OK as long as I can do it my way."

CHAPTER FIFTEEN

RELIGION AND POLITICS

I n our post 9/11 world no two words have as much meaning, or garner as much spirited debate. There are those who say this is precisely why we must have separation of church and state. Others say our culture will die without co-existence.

History tells us that from the days in the Garden of Eden until now there always has been a co-existence and by the very nature of the two disciplines there always will be and must be. Religion is political and politics are religious.

One definition of religion is "any system of faith or worship."

One definition of politics is "the form or constitution of government."

Every religion has a form of government, and every government has a set of beliefs or faith on which it was founded.

I challenge every liberal, atheist, jurist, and ACLU adherent to take their ill-thought-out positions of separation of church (religion), and state to its ultimate conclusion. Without a set of rules of conduct, which by their very nature must be based on some set of beliefs, we will have anarchy.

You may not believe or agree with the Scriptures, the Old and New Testament, however no one has presented an alternative which carries with it the time-tested rules of conduct for a civilized society. I am reminded of two scriptures which address this issue.

Judges 21:25; "in those days there was no king in Israel; every man did what was right in his own eyes." Change the word king to moral authority, which was what the king was to provide, and you have a better understanding of our current problem. To correct the situation God sent Judges to judge his people.

Psalms 2:1-3; "why do the nations conspire, and the peoples plot in vain? ---Let us burst their bonds asunder, and cast their cords from us." Unrestrained and unaccountable life styles are unacceptable in any society.

When you teach children, they came from slime or apes and that there are no absolutes of right and wrong you have children killing, stealing, and destroying without "feelings" of wrongdoing. And if as an adult, you still believe we evolved from whatever, you may be educated beyond your intellect.

The problem lies in this fact. "In the beginning, God created man in His, (God's), image." When man disobeyed his creator, he, man, recreated his god in his, (man's), image. Whenever man feels uncomfortable about being accepted by his god, he simply redesigns his god or changes gods. This is why we have so many religions and denominations. The answer lies in this fact. God never established a religion or denomination. Religion is simply man's attempt to do something to be accepted by God so man can take credit for his efforts. God desires a relationship with his greatest creation, man, and He has a plan for us to follow to form that relationship through a Redeemer, not a religion.

CHAPTER SIXTEEN

CHRISTIANITY MEANS CHRIST LIKE

So, what is the conclusion of the matter?

First let us state the truth. God is able to find those whose hearts are pure, who love Him and who have accepted Jesus Christ as their savior. It makes no difference what Church they belong to, or attend, as long as they have and continue to follow this admonition:

Romans 10:8 But what saith it? The word is nigh thee, even in thy mouth, and in thy heart: that is, the word of faith, which we preach;

Romans 10:9 That if thou shalt confess with thy mouth the Lord Jesus, and shalt believe in thine heart that God hath raised him from the dead, thou shalt be saved.

Romans 10:10 For with the heart man believeth unto righteousness; and with the mouth confession is made unto salvation.

Rom 10:11 For the scripture saith, Whosoever believeth on him shall not be ashamed.

I realize there are good people in all denominations who may disagree with this, because of teaching they have had from their youth, but it must be said again. Christianity is not a religion! Neither God nor Jesus Christ ever set up a Religion or Denomination, From the earliest writings of Genesis on, this has always been about a Relationship each person needs to have with God the Father, God the Son, and God the Holy Spirit, period.

Whether you are a Catholic, or Protestant, or a member of a fringe group who tries to follow Christ, you are still required to establish this personal relationship with God through Jesus Christ.

Amazingly God sifts through all the foolishness of man's creations, finds the good and continues on toward the end He alone sees and proclaims. So how should we live in the here and now? Here is a prayer the Lord gave me in 1998.

Help me Lord, today, to help someone else along their way; to give them hope when all seems lost, to strengthen and encourage each life storm tossed; to show your love by caring, to give myself in sharing, and to reflect your love so all can see, I am just being to them, what you have been to me.

Here is that salvation prayer again, you can use to give your life to God through Jesus.

Lord Jesus, I confess I am a sinner, I ask you to forgive my sins, to cleanse me of all unrighteousness, and to receive me into your family, the family of God. I believe you paid the price for my sins by your death on the cross, and that our Father God raised you from the dead, to be our forever Savior. Thank you, Lord Jesus, Amen.

See you in Heaven
John

P.S: When Paul and Silas were thrown into prison for preaching the Good News of Jesus as the Messiah, the Lord sent an earthquake to open the prison doors.

Acts 16:25 And at midnight Paul and Silas prayed, and sang praises unto God: and the prisoners heard them.

Acts 16:26 And suddenly there was a great earthquake, so that the foundations of the prison were shaken: and immediately all the doors were opened, and every one's bands were loosed.

Acts 16:27 And the keeper of the prison awaking out of his sleep, and seeing the prison doors open, he drew out his sword, and would have killed himself, supposing that the prisoners had been fled.

Acts 16:28 But Paul cried with a loud voice, saying, Do thyself no harm: for we are all here.

Acts 16:29 Then he called for a light, and sprang in, and came trembling, and fell down before Paul and Silas,

Acts 16:30 And brought them out, and said, Sirs, what must I do to be saved?

Acts 16:31 And they said, Believe on the Lord Jesus Christ, and thou shalt be saved, and thy house. Now that is pretty simple, isn't it? Believe and receive! Just don't add any junk!